24 STEPS TO GET A PROMOTION!

24 WAYS TO GET THE PROMOTION YOU DESERVE TO MAKE MORE MONEY!

Phil Johnson

Copyright © 2015 by D/O Publishing

Introduction

Welcome! Thanks a lot for joining me! Clearly if you picked up this book, you're interested in getting promoted. There can be a thousand reasons why you want to be promoted, but the two that are probably most important to people is making more money and getting more power.

Why more money? Because living is expensive! You have to pay your rent or mortgage, your car payment, food, gas, utilities, student loans and at the end of that, try to treat yourself to something more than a five dollar movie. Most people always need more money. More is never enough! Why? Well when we get a raise, we get used to the money increase and we spend more because we have more, then we need more so we can have more and so on and so forth! It's a vicious cycle.

For example, I remember working a minimum wage job at a music shop. Sure, it was commission based, but I rarely made more than minimum wage. I somehow found a way to pay for all my bills and squeak a little bit extra for small things to entertain me. Then I got a job at a company that paid me nearly three times as much! I thought to myself, "I'll have plenty of money! I can put some away, quickly pay off my debts and finally be happy!"

Sure, I got a lot more money. My paychecks were huge. I started investing my paycheck in a 401k and company stock. I was paying bills, and I was finally ahead for the first time in my life. Then I decided I wanted to buy a guitar I couldn't exactly afford… so I put it on credit. Then I wanted a newer, nicer car… Then I wanted to get my wife the best gifts… Then I used more credit because I thought, "well I'm making the big bucks!" Then my bills became staggered, and then I felt as tight as I did when I worked for minimum wage.

I know what you're thinking! Maybe I just need to get better at managing my money… I totally agree with you… But believe or not, more people than not live life this way. You might even live this way! I'm not judging. Life is too short to work paycheck to paycheck.

So short of getting hit by a car and collecting bonkers amount of cash from the insurance, or winning the lottery, really your only chance of making more money is getting a promotion.

Hopefully in the company you work for, there is room to move up and that the promotion you receive is more than just a few cents. I see so many people work at companies for years, and they only make a dollar or two more an hour than they did when they started. That's not a lot of money. That becomes extremely demotivating. If you're in that type of job, don't waste your time trying to get promoted. Find a job that will pay you what your worth!

A lot of people are afraid to leave their jobs in fear they won't find a job. There are a lot of good paying jobs out there, so go find them. Once you get in, that's when you'll want to read this book. For those of you who already have a good job at a good company and see real potential in growth, read forward! We're going to get you there.

Now, money might not be the only reason you want to get promoted. Maybe you like having power... a little extra responsibility. There's nothing wrong with that either. Some people just like being the boss! Making all the big decisions and being responsible for all the good things that come to the company. If anything, getting into the position of power can only strengthen the resume. If there were ever a time you wanted to switch jobs, having an upper management position would only help your case!

This book will have a ton of suggestions that I will flesh out. You need to take them seriously! There will be things in here where I know you'll roll your eyes. If you do roll your eyes, that will be the reason you won't get a promotion. Every job I've ever worked at, I found a way to get promoted within a year. I used a lot of the strategies I'm going to give you here.

If you follow these steps, you will get promoted. It's not a matter of if, it's a matter of when! With that being said, fasten your seatbelt and let's dive in!

Chapter 1: Look at Your Job

Before we dive into the nitty-gritty, I want you to follow me a little bit. We're going to jump into the job your working at first. Whether it's retail, sales, management or whatever else there is, think about this for a second:

- **Why did you get this job?**
- **How did you get your job?**
- **Does it pay you well enough?**
- **Is this a company you plan to stay in 5 years from now?**
- **Do you like the people you work with?**
- **Do you like the job you're doing?**

Before getting promoted, you need to make sure your heart is in it. So let's take each of these topics and go a little deeper.

Why did you get this job? Was this a job you actually wanted or something that you just saw in passing? Was it truly something you wanted to do, or just another 'job?'

When I worked at the music shop, I was convinced that the only other company I wanted to work for was this fancy FORTUNE 500 computer company. I used their products heavily, and I heard how great it was to work for them. I heard their pay was amazing; they had fantastic health benefits, and their products were somewhat of a passion for me. I wanted nothing but to work for them!

How did you get your job? Were you recommended by a friend? Did you apply in person or online? Did you bump into a manager who told you he could use someone like you?

If you had to go in for an interview, what was the process like? Were you dressed up with business casual clothes? Did you wear a suit and tie? How about a dress if you're a lady? Why do you think you were hired? Did they just hire anyone off the street, or was it a coveted position that a lot of people were gunning for?

A friend of mine that worked for the computer company gave my resume to his hiring manager. When I went to the 'interview' the computer company was holding, I discovered that it was actually a massive recruitment event. They had 50 new applicants in a room. We were separated into groups and did some activities to see how we worked together. Sadly, I wasn't called back for a second interview.

So I applied a second time. I was invited to a second hiring event. I passed and went on to a second interview. I wore khaki pants, a polo shirt, and nice shoes. They preferred we were comfortable in our skin when we interviewed.

I wasn't called back. I applied again. Same process and again I wasn't called back. I applied AGAIN and this time I got to the third interview. I didn't get a callback.

I applied the fifth and final time! I told myself if they didn't want me this time; they never will. They skipped me passed the hiring event and put me in an interview with one manager and two other applicants. I crushed it. My experience in these interviews was the reason I did so well. I went to a final interview with two managers, and I was so at ease because I was so familiar with the process, I came off comfortable and they hired me on the spot.

Does your job pay well enough? Is it sufficient to pay the bills or do you have enough to spend some and put some away in savings?

Again, I was coming from a minimum wage job, so when they hired me, I made nearly three times more, plus the best benefits in the business. From the very beginning, I knew I'd be happy with them.

Is your company one you plan to stay with five years from now? Be honest with yourself on this. Do you come home and complain about working there? Are you inspired? Is this a place where you feel valued and feel like you're a contributor to the company's success? Do you believe in the company and what they stand for?

The computer company offered so many benefits early in my career that it easily kept me interested in working for them five years out. They were a very profitable company, and they weren't afraid to flaunt it. They didn't take profits and horde them. They consistently put out higher living raises and gave out free products. There's room to grow in the company as well. There were four moves I could make on my way up. I started in sales. So I started at sales person and then I could move onto Head sales person, Manager, Senior Manager, Head Store Manager. There were a lot of positions outside of sales and management I could take as well.

Do you like the people you work with? Are they friends or are they just coworkers? Do you hang out outside of work? Do you have meaningful conversations beyond the usual work mumbo jumbo?

One of the best things about my job was that everyone I worked with was amazing. I got along with everybody. All of us would hang out after work. We supported each other in our personal lives as well as our careers. It felt like a big family. I've worked at plenty of places where this normally was not the case. Still, it's something you should note in your place of employment. It's ok to be friends with the people you spend half your time with.

Do you like the job you're doing? Think honestly for a second. Is it easy for you? Do you feel challenged? Is it fun or is it pointless to you?

I honestly loved my job. I was paid very well to talk to people. I got to play with the newest gadgets and learn about them before anybody. I got to change people's lives when they walked into our store. It wasn't very hard, but I was able to challenge myself all the time with my development.

So answer these questions honestly. If you can't seem to find a lot of positives in your answers, maybe gunning for a promotion won't be a solution to the bigger problem. I read somewhere once that if you've been with a company for two years and you haven't received a promotion, it may be time to move on. However, if you do like your job, at least enough to keep working for them, then we can move forward.

Chapter 2: The Basics

So if you've made it this far, that means you really want to move up in this company. It's easy just to say "I want a promotion" but what does that mean exactly to you? What is the reason?

When I started at the computer company, my sales were off the charts. My manager noticed immediately and told me he saw big things happening for me. They had a head of sales position, so I decided I wanted to do that. The pay was a modest income boost. I made that my goal.

A goal needs to be written down. You need to be able to look at it on a daily basis and see it. Keeping it in your head won't do anyone any good. You need tangible evidence!

Get a Journal

In your journal, you want to be sure to write down your goals. The goal could be something like "become assistant manager by July 1st." Make sure the time you allot yourself is realistic. If you just started at your job, clearly setting a goal like "In one week, I'll be promoted" won't be very likely. Make it realistic and stick by it.

Every day you work, make a plan for yourself. Make it something measurable. In our store, we had 'metrics.' We had to sell extended warranties. So I would write down "get 60% warranty attachment by the end of the day." If I hit it, I was doing something right, and I could write my experiences down. If I hadn't, I could measure and see where my opportunities lie.

The goals aren't the only reason to have a journal. You can write about interactions, new learns, and a ton of other experiences you have on the job. Then when it comes time to interview, you have a huge notebook full of examples that you can share to give yourself the best chance of getting promoted!

Arrive Early

One simple thing you can do to give yourself a 100% better chance of getting promotion is getting to work on time. I think the saying goes, "To be early is to be on time and to be on time is to be late…" Being on time can be one of the simplest things you can do. You ultimately have all the control on if you arrive early.

If you're guilty of getting to work right on time, or even a couple minutes late, you need to make a drastic change right now. Speaking from managerial experience, if a person was consistently late, I took it as they didn't respect their job or the team they worked with, so they would be at the bottom of my list when it came time to look for new candidates.

Set your alarm fifteen minutes earlier and start your day at that moment. Always give yourself an extra cushion of time in case there is a car accident on the way to work. I've implemented this simple step and in the last six years that I've worked with the company, I have been late only once. It was by five minutes. The Reason? The President of the United States was coming into town, so a huge squad of police cars, secret service SUVS, and other protective vehicles ultimately took over the interstate and drove at a very slow rate.

I live half an hour away from work, and I always leave 50 minutes early. With the technology being as accessible as it is, it's very easy to look up if traffic is going to be a problem. The very first thing I do when I wake up is check my smartphone to see if there are any accidents that I need to avoid. I have three different ways I can take to get to work. Make a map and stick to it!

Stay Late

If your boss asks you to stay late and you have nothing going on in your life after work, stay a bit. Putting in a little extra time can go a long way with a boss. It's a "you scratch my back, I'll scratch yours" kind of thing.

There is a limit that you want to do this because sadly some people will take advantage of you. If you do have plans and can't stay late, don't feel bad about saying no. We are scheduled and shouldn't be expected to stay beyond those hours (unless of course you're on salary… then sorry about that…).

I'm a strong believer in a work/life balance but let's face it, if you don't have a life, make some extra money and better your situation while you have the time!

Smile and be happy

This is probably one of those "roll your eyes" moments, but seriously you need to smile and be happy that you have the privilege to work at your company. They could have picked anybody, but they picked you. Make sure they don't regret that decision.

Every time I go to work, I do everything I can to leave my negativity at the door and look to enjoy myself at work. I'm changing lives!

Smiling goes a long way. I work with plenty of people who look miserable. They clearly don't like their job, and they're not happy to be there. And you know what? They never get promoted. The ones who tend to move up are the ones who put in the most effort; the ones who are glad to do anything. The ones that come in and make the work environment a better place because they are happy to be there. Be that type of person, and you'll get good things!

Don't. Do. Drama.

Stay the hell away from it. All managers look for those who spread wildfires. If you're a person who gets worked up over other people's problems and talks about them with everybody, you can be sure you won't be trusted.

I worked with a guy who was #1 in sales, had fantastic customer surveys and knew everything about everything. He was by far our most valuable sales asset. His goal was that he wanted to be a manager. Sadly, all those wonderful things he was able to do couldn't save his job.

He would regularly spread rumors, or share confidential information with people that shouldn't have known it. The leaks would ultimately lead back to him. If his managers gave him some developmental coaching, he would throw it back in their face and focus on their flaws. Needless to say, it didn't matter how good he did for the business, he was a terrible drama starter, and it ultimately led to his firing.

The moral of the story is to stay away from it. Focus on the things that matter and ignore the things that don't!

Look the Part!

How can anyone begin to take you seriously if you don't look like you take yourself seriously. You should always come to work looking presentable, with non-wrinkled clothes, presentable hair cut… you know, the works!

The ones who look like losers will continue to be losers. You should take pride in all aspects of your job but most importantly, take pride in yourself. There are plenty of jobs that are loose with the dress code, but don't take advantage of it. That could be the difference between you getting a promotion and not getting a promotion. Seem like a stupid thing? When it comes down to it, I'm more interested in who cares more. If I have two equally fantastic employees that deserve this job, it's the little things I have to nitpick to find out whose the best. Looking sloppy could be the difference!

These may seem obvious, but there are so many people that overlook these steps, so It's my duty that I leave no stone unturned. You have got to learn to walk before you learn to run.

Remember to start with the little things first. As you manage to grasp these ideas, you can move on and become more valuable as time moves on,

Chapter 3: The Next Level

So now that we got the basics out of the way let's look at other ways that you can help yourself by getting that promotion! This chapter is really focusing on your actions being seen and heard. If no one knows you're working towards something, what's going to make them pay attention? Some people have so many things going on in their own lives, that they might not notice without your help.

Find a Mentor

If you're looking at a position, maybe it's time to talk to someone who knows something about it. Perhaps someone who currently holds the position or held it in the past.

Make that person your mentor. Ask them questions about their experiences. Ask them everything from what they did to prepare for the role, the types of questions they had to answer in the interview, etc. It's an excellent opportunity to find out the pros and cons of the position so that you can find a way to tailor your strengths towards it.

Ask them to keep an eye on you and give you pointers. If you can get their buy in, it's possible it could lead to goo things later.

You never know what kind of relationship they have with the hiring manager. Maybe they'll say something about you approaching them and finding ways to better yourself. Sometimes "it's not what you know, but who you know..." Talk to them as often as you can and use them as a measuring stick. Find out how long it took them to get the position and the small breakthroughs they made to ultimately get them ready.

I promise if you're not asking them the questions, your competition will.

Get New Knowledge or Acquire a New skill

As perfect as we all like to think we are, the simple fact is some of us are more skilled than others at all types of different situations. But just because you're not skilled doesn't mean you can't be!

Get your journal ready on this step and talk to your mentor, manager, or look up the requirements for the job that you want. Read between the lines. Don't look at just what the job entails, but rather what skills they'd like you to have in order for you to be successful.

When I went to be Head of Sales, I read that I was going to need to be able to flex some leadership skills. I was great at sales, and I had great relationships with my co-workers but between you and me, I was kind of a goofball. I overused my humor skill a bit. So when it came time for people to take me seriously like a boss, it was hard to imagine.

So I took baby steps. I picked up an FYI: For Your Improvement book and looked at the competencies that made up a good leader. I needed to be more than just good at my job. I needed to be able to have buy-in from my team. So I looked at the newest people on the team, and I started with them. I would ask how they felt in their current role and asked if there were ways I could support them. I would have "extra" conversations that were out of the scope of my role, but it helped give me the confidence to have those same conversations with my peers.

It took a couple months but people used me heavily as a resource and saw me as someone they could come to. It took practice, and I had to identify it to work on it. Not everybody is going to go out of their way to tell you what you need to do to be great. Sometimes you have to do the legwork yourself. But I'm glad I was able to do it myself because I learned a new skill in self-development.

Don't work for the Job You Have… Work for the Job You Want

In your current role, you're probably skilled enough in it to make your boss happy. If not, you'd be fired. You should never be content with what you have. Always be hungry for more. If you did the research in the last step and discovered you don't have the skills necessary to get the job you seek, what do you do? Roll over and die? Hell no! You develop. You learn those skills and you practice them daily, keeping track of it every step of the way in your journal.

When that position comes around, you want everybody to think that that position belongs to you. Not just management, but your peers as well.

I remember when I was just a lowly sales guy on the sales floor at the computer company. As I began to develop, my peers saw me in a new light. Management asked for my humble opinion on scenarios. I remember when the position was offered to me and announced to the store, everyone said "wait, I thought you already were Head of Sales? I made believers out of everybody. How? I went above and beyond my current role. It doesn't take that much to separate yourself from the pack.

Ask for More Responsibilities

The difference between someone who's going places to someone who's not is their work ethic. Are you the type of person who takes a little extra work as a challenge, or someone who sees it as a burden? Learning to develop yourself is clearly an excellent way to take things to the next level but don't just focus on yourself. Ask people around you if you can lend an extra hand. Ask if you can do some of the responsibilities that are required of upper management (assuming you're allowed). You want the ball! You know if you can do it, the job will get done right! If you can take a little extra work off the hands of your co-workers and raise morale a bit, why not? *Make note of it in your journal.

Don't Expect to be Rewarded!

Even with you doing all this extra work, the ultimate goal is to get the promotion, so don't focus on being rewarded for every little extra thing you do.

Just imagine that they're keeping a list with gold stars and that those will add up to a sizable promotion!

Take your job to a whole new level... and leave it there!

One mistake that a lot of people tend to make is they will work really hard for a short amount of time with hopes that they'll get what they want, and then they'll take their foot off the gas and go back to their old ways. We don't want that. You're going to be different.

Don't just ask for extra tasks one day, or develop for one day and quit! You want the pedal to the floor the whole time. Develop daily! Do additional tasks every day! You want to push and work as hard as you can. Imagine when you get that promotion. Are you going to work less hard? That doesn't make sense... You need to get the momentum up and keep it going!

TEAMWORK

In business, you cannot go in with a ME ME ME mentality. It won't work, and no one will trust you. You have to think about what you can bring to the team. How can you make everybody else's job easier with hopes that they'll want to do the same for you. Even if they don't, you make their job easier because that's what's going to get you promoted!

When we look at what we've done so far, even though I spent the time developing myself, I used the skills I developed to help develop others which only makes the team better. There's nothing selfish about that.

Keep track in your journal about how you're helping the team. Document each conversation, each task and everything in between. Have all those stories at the ready to talk about.

Don't skip the Office Party!

When it comes to giving yourself a fighting chance for a position, you want to make sure you're networking at any opportunity. One of the best ways to do this is at an office party. Usually all of upper management is required to attend these, so you have an excellent opportunity to meet, introduce yourself and talk candidly with them. You may learn something you never knew which could help you relax when it comes to interviewing!

Let Management Know What You're Working Towards!

In order to have buy-in from management, they have to know what I'm working towards. When I set a goal, I make sure to let everyone know. My peers, my friends, my mentor and of course management.

I make sure to remind them on a weekly basis. Not by just knocking on their door and giving useless information, but with examples from my journal. I would tell them about an interaction that I thought would help me in my development towards the position I wanted.

Management talks with each other. You need to leave no doubt that you are, indeed, the right person for the job... But with that being said:

NO BROWN NOSING

For those of you who don't know, brown nosing is a term for those who kiss their manager's butts. They suck up to them, laugh at all their crummy jokes, and really take away the pride in getting a promotion. I'm sure you've seen it before. When brown nosing works for someone, it really takes the air out of your sails, but don't result to it. You put in the hard work and follow the other steps, and you'll get the job you deserve, along with a bunch of extra skills.

Establish a Good Relationship With Your Boss!

Having a good relationship and brown nosing are two very different things. With brown nosing, there's a sense of dishonesty. You're not genuine. When you establish a good relationship with your boss, they'll invest in you.

Ask them questions about how they got started and the journey they took. Much like a mentor, find everything you can about them and share equally with them.

Any time I began working at a new place, I always made sure to have a good relationship with management. I wanted them to know what I was about, and I wanted to know what they were about. I didn't want anybody to misread information. Plus, once they know you, that builds trust, and trust goes a long way when it comes to bumping someone up to a new position.

Chapter 4: The Top Level

In this chapter, we're going to cover some steps that will ask a little more of you. There will be a mix of some things you can do in and outside of the office. That doesn't mean you need to wash your boss's car (check brown nosing...) but if your job is a large part of your life, you don't only have to think of ways to develop yourself within the walls of your company.

READ!

What's nice about this step is that you're already doing it! There are hundreds of precious books that you can help you in your development! It can be all different parts of your job. If there's a book about a position that even remotely reminds you of the one you want, read that and take every bit of information that you can from it!

I mentioned the FYI For Your Improvement book earlier. It deals with Lominger Competency talk. It's a $150 book. Gigantic, very expensive, but very useful. Once I learned how to read it and applied it to my job, I saw the type of results I never thought possible.

There are so many inexpensive resources out there, and I highly recommend that you invest in couple books for yourself. Honestly, the more you have your mind on your goal, the better off you'll be!

*If you're a sales person who needs a little extra help, check out my book **STAY HUMAN: THE 8 STEPS TO BECOMING A SALES ROCKSTAR**

Challenge your boss

Ultimately when it comes to your superior, we have to remember that they are a normal person just like you and me. Like us, they make mistakes, and it's ok for them to be called out on it. Now I'm not saying you need to rub it in their face when they make a mistake. I REALLY don't recommend that. You have to be very delicate with this step because if you overstep your boundaries, you may find yourself looking for a new job altogether.

If your boss makes a mistake, you want to approach it with a solution. Instead of saying something blatantly stupid like "YOU'RE WRONG," you want to focus more on "Hey, I noticed you mentioned this, but I found that if you look at this, your conclusion would actually be this..." If you come from a solution point of view, it's less hostile, and it builds good rapport with them. Feeling comfortable with management will only work to your advantage as you grow with the company.

If You Have Bad News, Bring a Solution!

To add on to challenging your boss, really anytime there's a problem in your job, you don't want to state the obvious and leave it at that. Moments like these are where you can separate yourself from the pack.

In the computer store, the entire team was having trouble selling extended warranties to students because the perception was that the students didn't have enough money. Most people approached it with "They're students, they don't have the cash." If that's how most people dealt with their problems, nothing would ever get solved.

I was successful at positioning the extended warranties to students, so I took my skills and taught it out to those who were experiencing problems. I focused on building value and taking the price out of the equation. As I taught this out, the attachment rate went up three-fold. Then I had another story for the journal.

If you're a solution getter, management is going to want you in a better position. They want you to be able to think on your feet. They want you to be more self-sufficient, so they don't feel like they have to babysit you. Make sense? Good.

Show that You Can Receive Feedback!

It seems one of the hardest things to do is listen to someone tell you how to better yourself. Most of us tend to be very stubborn and expect negative intentions when someone gives it to us. You should absolutely welcome feedback!

It's important to listen and not interrupt. Even if you don't agree, perception is everything. If someone gives you feedback and tells you you're kind of a jerk, ask for examples. Those moments are perfect for learning something new.

You can take it a step further and ask your peers for feedback. People are more likely to share it if you're asking for it. Some folks are afraid of approaching someone with feedback for fear it may come off as hostile. Take that out of the equation and ask away. Ask someone to watch what you do on a working day and see where you can improve. Ask management to look as well. There's nothing more impressive than a person who is up to bettering themselves.

Don't forget to write those interactions in your journal!

Make a Deadline Personal

If your team is required to have something due at a certain time, take the lead. Make that deadline your own and hold others accountable. Of course, you should offer help where you can, but in group projects, if one person is late, everybody is late.

When I was a part of the head sales team, every week we were given "assignments" that we had to have ready by the next meeting. In this particular case, we were supposed to pick one person on the sales team, identify their opportunities and have a conversation with them about it.

I worked very hard on mine, had a great conversation, and prepared a 5-minute presentation to talk about it with my team. Well, three of the six members didn't finish in time. Our manager wrote us all a nasty email saying that we failed, and none of us did what we were told. I was infuriated by that, so I went and talked with my manager and showed that I had indeed done my work and worked very hard on it. She told me that maybe I should have checked on my team since it was a group exercise.

From that day on, anytime we were given an assignment, I was on top of everybody like white on rice. I made sure everyone was ready and held each and every one of them accountable. Our meetings became more productive, and I was seen as a leader on that team after that.

So whether it's just you or an entire team's deadline, make it personal and make sure the time limit is reached with significant results!

Chapter 5: The Interview

After you've used these steps in some form and fashion, you will eventually get an opportunity to interview for the position. To get an interview is a big feat! If you make it this far, you must be proud of what you accomplished, and no matter what happens, you are moving in the right direction.

Prepare for the interview

So assuming you've followed every step thus far in this book, you're going to have a journal full of interactions, experiences and goals that you've gathered over the last several months. The first thing you need to do is read through the entire thing. That's right. Everything. You'll be surprised how clearly the interactions you had in the past come back to you. You'll remember them like they happened yesterday.

Once you've read, pick the best interactions or experiences that match the following topics:

- **Tell us about a time where you had to give tough feedback.**
- **Tell us about a time where you positively influenced the team.**
- **Tell us about a time where you had a deadline to reach. How did you go about meeting it on time?**
- **Tell us about the time where you had a conflict and how did you solve it?**

You're going to get asked a lot of situational questions, and you want to make sure that you have a ton of answers and scenarios at the ready because every interview is a little different. Think about what you bring to the table. Be prepared to talk about your skills, the skills you've acquired over the last few months, as well as a few of your opportunities. Most importantly get a good night's sleep. Never underestimate the power of getting your 8 hours!

The Interview

The interview will probably be the most stressful part of the entire process but if you nail it, you'll get more money and more responsibility, IE POWER!

Sell yourself!

No one is going to know every single thing you've done to get yourself ready for this position. Sure, there will be pieces that people see, but you got a whole notebook full of life changing moments. Talk about it! Sell yourself! Be confident! You've done everything you can do and plus some! You have proof! Most people can't go into an interview with that kind of evidence, and that's where you'll have the advantage.

Your interview will be the last shot you can take to convince them that you are the right person for the job, so don't hold back. Look the interviewer in the eye, have your stories ready and DON'T ANSWER A QUESTION UNTIL YOU KNOW THE ANSWER!

I have failed some interviews because I was afraid to let there be silence when a question was asked that I didn't have a prepared answer for. So I would just start talking, and half way through the mumbo jumbo, I would figure out the point I was trying to make, change directions and end on something completely different from where I started.

Talk about anything and everything, what you can bring to the table, what you hope to learn in the position and show your passion. Every interview I've ever had, I've been thanked for my passion for the team.

Talk about yourself, but make sure that you ultimately tie it to the good of the team. "Over the last several months, I've been able to learn some leadership skills that has positively impacted the team on the sales floor. I've successfully given feedback, coaching and because of that, metrics is on the rise. I believe in this new role, I can utilize my strengths that can only help the team succeed further."

In the interview, make it known you want the job. You are a professional, and you deserve it. However, if there is tough competition, you need to make sure you don't oversell the position to yourself. Just in case...

Sorry, You didn't get the job...

For every three interviews I have, I only get one promotion. You can look at it in one of two ways... You suck... or it's a learning experience. Every interview I've ever had, I've taken something from it and used it in the next interview. Remember my example at the beginning of the book. It had taken me five different hiring processes before I was finally hired. If I had given up, I would probably still be working at a minimum wage job with little ambition. I took every experience as a glass half full situation and went back armed with experience.

If you don't get the job, ask for feedback from the managers if you can. Ask how you presented yourself in the interview and if there were ways that you could have improved. Don't be hostile. Sometimes you're not right for the job at that time, or there is someone else more qualified. That's OK. You keep doing the steps in this book, and then the next time you'll crush it and you'll forget all about the first interview.

Managers gauge how people react after not being hired. If you're sour and unpleasant, they will make note of that, and it could hurt all future chances of you getting the position.

I once applied to be a trainer in our store. It was an experience that if I had gotten it, I would get to spend six months training. It was a position I wasn't sure how to prepare for because every trainer in the past had a drastically different approach. My interview was pleasant enough. I got along with the managers, had good conversations, and it ended friendly. I noticed I hadn't prepared any ideas how I would change the system. How would I be innovative?

They ended up hiring another gentleman who ended up being amazing. He did things with the position no one had done before and, as a result, the store did better. I looked at his experience and made the mental note that I couldn't have done what he did, had I had gone first. After seeing what he did, if I applied again I would be so much more effective.

I shared this insight with my managers, and they applauded the personal insight. It's ok to lose because it helps you learn to win.

Congratulations, You got the job!

You win! All your hard work paid off! You should feel proud of yourself. You put in the time, and somebody took notice and decided to give you a chance. The hard work isn't over. Now that you've reached your goal, it's not the time to road on cruise control. You need to work even harder and prove that management made the right choice.

After a couple months of getting the hang of your new job, you need to consider what your next major goal is? What's the next level? Do you want to stay in your current position and really dominate, or was it merely a stepping stone that was going to get you to your ultimate goal?

In my case, I managed to get Head Sales but my real goal was Manager. So I repeated the steps in this book. I found the competencies that are related to that position, and I challenged myself all over again, constantly looking for new skills.

The important part is that you don't give up. Even if you move all the way to CEO, you must keep yourself accountable. Always be hungry for more and continually learn new skills.

Conclusion

Hopefully in this guide, you've learned how to organize your approach to getting a promotion. It doesn't matter what kind of field your in, you can take these approaches and scale them in any format. Just stay organized and keep records of your goals.

Remember your self-worth and if there's no valid path for growth, don't waste your time. Find a company that can give you the ability to move up. You're more than just a paycheck. Always feel challenged and always be hungry for more. You owe it to yourself!

Before I worked at the computer company, I worked at the music store for nearly two years. I worked so hard to get promoted to department manager. The increase in pay was so little, and the stress increased by so much more. I knew at that moment that I was better than what they had to offer me, and I changed my situation.

Some of these steps will take you several months to implement, but what's most important is that you have patience. Hopefully, you'll live a long life and learn new things every day! Stay the course, and you'll make it!

Check out these other books brought to you by D/O PUBLISHING!

http://www.amazon.com/dp/B00U2WP4H0

STAY HUMAN: THE 8 STEPS TO BECOMING A SALES ROCKSTAR by **Phil Johnson**

STAY HUMAN: THE 8 STEPS TO BECOMING A SALES ROCKSTAR is a fantastic guide that will give you the tools you need to get started as a sales person

Are you new to sales? Are you having trouble hitting sales goal or making connections with your customers? You're not alone. There are a lot of sales people out there but for every good salesman there is, there 9 others that aren't. You don't have to be a part of that unskilled pool of talent.

In this book we'll go through 8 steps that will help analyze your interactions, give you tips and exercises to practice so that you'll be a top ranked salesperson in no time!

STAY HUMAN
The book focuses on taking the emphasis off selling a product and focusing on being genuine to build a connection

HOW TO NAVIGATE INTERACTIONS

We go through everything from the first impression to the final goodbye, setting you up for the best success!

DIFFERENT SCENARIOS
We break down different types of interactions and point at what to look for.

If you're just getting started, or need a fresher in the most practical sales techniques, look no further than STAY HUMAN: THE 8 STEPS TO BECOMING A SALES ROCKSTAR

HOW TO THINK LIKE A MILLIONAIRE: TIPS AND TRICKS TO BE MORE PRODUCTIVE AND MAKE BIG MONEY! By **Phil Johnson**
http://www.amazon.com/dp/B00V1QANCW

All we want is to be rich! We want enough money to pay for all of our desires and live a luxurious life with little to no effort. The sad part is that unless you win the lottery, or inherit some money from a wealthy relative, it's not just going to fall into your lap. You have to work for it!

Through out this book, we will explore the thinking of a millionaire and ways that you can adapt so that you can motivate yourself to become more!

We'll reference some of the world's most known millionaires (and some billionaires) while calling you to action to get up and change your life.

What are you waiting for?! Hit the download button now and change your mindset now!

http://www.amazon.com/dp/B00U5QA88S

WAKE UP AND GO! A GUIDE TO GET YOUR LIFE BACK by **Matthew Newton**

WAKE UP AND GO! A GUIDE TO GET YOUR LIFE BACK is all in the title. Are you caught in a rut? Feel like you're going in circles and never seem to find happiness? In this guide, we will break down whats pulling you down, and find new ways to rebuild yourself!

LOOK AT YOUR LIFE
We will analyze what's right in wrong at this current moment in time

LOOK AT YOUR LOVE LIFE
Whether you're in a relationship or not, we will get down to the fundamentals and find ways to revitalize your love life!

WHO DO YOU WANT TO BE?
We will take a look at all things that you dreamed of being but used excuses to avoid trying for.

DISCONNECT AND RECONNECT
We will cut ties with the ones the bring us down and we'll give you tips to reconnect with the "friends for a lifetime"

CAREER

We will analyze your job and career ambitions and find ways to improve them or start over all together!

STOP BUYING POSSESSIONS... MAKE MEMORIES
Instead of spending countless dollars on things that will ultimately never be used or break, we find a way to plan a trip of a life time.

AND SO MUCH MORE...

If you need help or guidance on what to do, read this book, do the exercises, and get your life back!